Hymnal

Julia Bell is a writer and academic. She is the author of novels, the bestselling *Creative Writing Coursebook* and the book-length essay *Radical Attention*. Her essays and short stories have been published nationally and internationally including in the *TLS*, the *White Review* and the *Paris Review* and broadcast on the BBC. Her poetry has been longlisted for the National Poetry Competition and the Bridport Prize. She is a Reader in Creative Writing at Birkbeck, University of London.

Hymnal

Julia Bell

PARTHIAN

Parthian, Cardigan SA43 1ED
www.parthianbooks.com
First published in 2023
© Julia Bell 2023
ISBN 978-1-914595-11-0
Editor: Susie Wildsmith
Cover design by Emily Courdelle
Typeset by Elaine Sharples
Printed and bound by 4edge Limited, UK
Published with the financial support of the Welsh Books Council
British Library Cataloguing in Publication Data
A cataloguing record for this book is available from the British Library
Printed on FSC accredited paper

Hymnal is provided to selected libraries across Wales with support of The Borzello Trust
to promote the reading of contemporary poetry by new and emerging voices.

You sat in the stone church;
To what secret prayers
Did your lips say, Amen?
– R.S. Thomas

CONTENTS

ABERYSTWYTH (1988–1989)

Glossary
Acknowledgements
So many of the poems are exploded memories: An interview with Julia Bell

Preface

Late in the 1960s, before I was born, my father and mother visited Aberaeron, a small fishing town on the west coast of Wales. Here, my father heard a voice – which he knew to be God – directing him to minister to the Welsh. In the early 1970s, six months after I was born, we moved to Aberaeron where he took up his first curateship. Over the next eighteen years we would move to various parishes within a forty-mile radius: first to Llangeler a predominantly Welsh-speaking parish in the Teifi valley, then back to Aberaeron where my father became vicar, and then to a larger and more Evangelical church in Aberystwyth.

I have written this memoir in verse because it's how I remember. Snapshots in words strung along a line, which somehow constitute a life. Snapshots of another time from now, but from a time which tells me about how I got here. Not the whole story, but my story. Of an English family on a mission from God, of signs and wonders in the Welsh countryside, of difference, and of faith and its loss.

BEFORE

Our Father

Did you hear it in the clang of the rigging?
The see-saw cawing of gulls,
the sight of the sea through the lips
of the harbour, like a kiss in your ears?

The blue sky rough as your cheeks,
flying high, full of life's electricity.
The kind of day in which I can imagine
God might speak, so much speaks of him already.

Did the voice echo from the walls,
still warm from the day's heat?
Weighted like a commandment –
Here is the path – walk in it.

You, the star of your own Bible story,
born-again Welshman, *pregethwr*,
anointed with the fire of the ancients
who carry their torches to Bethlehem on burning knees.

Pram

Crammed in under the blanket
is all you can see of me, little lamb,
and the two of you bending to look
as if into a wishing well.

Hunched in camel coat and headscarf,
into that big black hole of the pram
yourselves repeated beneath the blanket,
ticking loud as a bomb.

ABERAERON PART 1
(1971–1974)

Red Tea Set

Kept for best, and plastic as the fire of hell
that throbs behind my eyes, even when I sleep.
Here's a cup for Teddy,

milk and two sugars for Ragdolly Anne.
Mumbling, I work out what is fair,
and who's had more than their share.

Inside, people pray to God.
I am small and we are learning
how we do vicarage afternoons.
Bless, take care.

Ebol Fach

Little Donkey, little donkey
On a lonely road. Or is it dusty?
Or something.
Perhaps it was *Kum bah yah*.

Little Donkey, little donkey,
Miserable Eeyore, with his
fleabitten hide, tied up
outside that farm in Plwmp.

Little Donkey, little donkey,
carrying Mary and Joseph,
and eventually Jesus, from Wales
to our dreamtime Middle East.

Little Donkey, little donkey,
on the red frame with wheels.
Pushed by me, cutie pie,
golden apple of his eye.

LLANGELER
(1974–1980)

Llangeler Sunday, 1974

Eager for the new vicar
are Rhiannon and Lizzie Anne,
resplendent in their floral Sundays.

The pedal organ wheezes
as Mair with the stout legs
shows off through the hymnal.

She took a ride on a pedallo once, in Italy,
with a handsome gondolier
willing her dreams around the horseshoe bay.

I wonder if she thinks of it now
as she pumps up the volume on
the 'Rock of Ages'.

And there you are up the front
with your John the Baptist hair
and trendy flares

and a new language learns your mouth
like the crags of a swallowed
mountain, a borrowed flame.

National Eisteddfod, Carmarthen, 1975

All day eating crisps in a bonnet.
Dressed like a Welsh lady,
I ride a bumpy Shetland pony, pet a goat,
my brother burbles in the pushchair,
it rains. How it rains.

We shelter in the tent with Nuclear Power
No Thanks and the fishy hippies,
and my mother is suspicious
of their New Age ways and vegan sandwiches.
Everything smells brown.

There are people riding horses,
women doing difficult things with a harp.
The grass is rough and tussocky.
And flags flap for the Welsh Nats
and their hard language.

Later, we watch livestock displayed:
sheep, rams, bullocks. Especially the bullocks,
herded by tense men with red cheeks
who look like grocers,
in stained green coats and flat caps.

Rough hands who reek of farms,
same as their fathers, and their fathers'
fathers, and their fathers before that,
right back to Owain Glyndŵr,
and before that the age of dragons.

These are the people we have come to tell,
they need to know they are going to hell.

Eyepatch

It has been discovered that I can't see
and need to have an operation.
Mother thinks I'm special needs.
There are tests.

We are in the world but not of it,
so I mustn't mind about the eyepatch and the specs,
and anyway we see, as if through a glass.
Darkly.

Visiting the People

*Behold I stand at the door and knock, if any man hear my voice, and open the
door, I will come in to him, and will sup with him, and he with me.*
Revelation 3:20

When Father took me with him, we were received.
Hunched parlours, kept for best and death and the vicar,
heavy furniture, the sneeze of dust. Gnarly hands offering boiled sweets.
Have you thought about your relationship with God?
I'm new here, we have a service—

Sometimes people started shouting.
Or they looked appalled. *Will there be guitars?*
If there are guitars I'm not coming.
Or they sat silently, weeping. Those were the worst.
Things have been so difficult, vicar, since my husband—

He learned who to call on, who to avoid. Who was Baptist,
Jehovah's Witness, Mormon, Catholic, bored. Who kept dogs.
Who was old and angry, who was questioning the Lord.
They were the ones he wanted: the sorrowful, the guilty,
the ignored. Softened by suffering, like Job.

He added them, like pennies for the missionaries.
Souls who walked in darkness, now bathing in the light
of all the angels and archangels, and me, the appeal,
cherub-cheeked, plied with sweets and fancy treats,
rattling the gifted coins in my pocket like a mendicant.

Llangeler Village School

The village school is two rooms
one for big and one for small.
In assembly once, I saw a mouse and screamed
in the middle of the Lord's Prayer
and there was pandemonium.

There are brown dinners in a long brown hall
with brown meat too chewy
for my delicate teeth.
Dinner ladies slop with swollen arms,
and everyone speaks Welsh.

Today they serve us something pink –
old school – luncheon meat.
I turn my nose up because
I don't want chewy gristle.
This refusal goes round the village

before they have rung the bell.
Even my mother has heard about it.
The fussy vicar's daughter
not knowing processed meat is soft,
and that's the point.

Language Lessons

And I don't remember how, at
Bryn Saron School, I bent my mouth around the sounds.
Copying children in the playground
Chware, with the hard walls of the throat.

Days passed in front of the blackboard, beneath *Y*
Ddraig Coch, which points its forked tongue at Miss
Evans, my teacher, who yesterday I mistook
For my mother.

Ffion's brother said she was a fucking cow.
Gyrru ar gyrru, clipti clop, clipti clop, fy
Ngheffyl ddu. All day. Songs about riding black
Horses and red dragons and white sheep.

Inside the words is a world of ancient intercessions,
Loud sounds in which the tongue slips, like
Llaeth, a harder, slippier word for milk. Or
Mwnci, swinging on the jungle gym.

Now we are counting, *un, dau, tri*, old as
Ogham, scratching on the stones, like
People tallying weeks in jail, Children! Use *ei*
Phen, Miss Evans taps her head often and then

Rhian needs the toilet, Wayne has made a
Smell. Home time nears. Mother asks me what I learned at school,
This and that, I say, and repeat what Ffion's brother
Thinks of Miss Evans. *Don't you dare*

Use that language in this house, young lady, you
Wash your mouth out, as
You well know, we only speak the words of God round here.

16

Summer 1976

Sadistic weather for the sack race:
the grass has died, the hedgerow burned.
Sych, like the word and its meaning, *parched*.

Afterwards, I have to lie down
in the back of the vergers' Volvo,
hallucinating, because of heatstroke.

There are men in bonnets acting out the Rebecca Riots.
The churchwarden's wife is in military uniform, her blackface
melting into her collar. Apparently, she is Idi Amin.

I feel sickly strange and suck a cola ice which melts before I eat it
and think about what Father said at Remembrance service.
We shall not see their like again.

The Left Behind

I have this dream a lot, I am locked all alone
in this yard with the lumpy tarmac
and mossy cracks and rusting jungle gym.

I am out of breath, panic boxing
my ears, running round and round
the playground, demented.

I have been forgotten, in this forsaken place.
Dread seeps, like the grey Welsh stone
and the drizzle.

Maybe it's the video on stranger danger
they showed us in assembly
where a girl got kidnapped from a graveyard

or maybe I dreamt that too.
And Father's fiery sermon on
the judgement that will happen when we die.

There is no way out, except to wake up
roaring, crying, breathing hard
to every beat of my unclean heart.

Gypsy Dancing

She is the kind of woman the 70s were invented for:
a body for disco chiffon and a head for scarves,
suntan all year round and so much jewellery she clatters.
She even has a glamorous name: Mrs Camden,
which speaks of London and of fashion, a world away
from this backward place and its rough children.
Disdain comes off her like the smoke from her Sobranies.

This year, she is organising the school production.
I am a gypsy dancer, sweeping with my broom
in some cheap choreographed moves designed to look cute.
Except I am not cute, I am the daughter of the vicar who

everyone says looks like Richard Chamberlain.
We sweep and sweep, first this way then that,
furrowing our frowns of concentration.
She is especially keen on shouting when I miss my cues.

The parents all have programmes and are seated in advance
amid a hush of expectation. Beginning our routine the brush
flies off my broom. Someone giggles. I search
between the legs of strangers and fix it back together.
But her formation is screwed and the cute gypsies are confused.
You didn't need the bloody brush – you should have pretended to sweep the floor!
It seems to me now that this remains my fatal flaw.

Machynlleth Holiday Cottage

A dark house with damp furniture,
and nature so close it could have crawled inside the windows.

Isn't it lovely to get away? Father said,
as the fire crept along the ridge of the valley.

And we watched it burn through the night
as if it had been lit just for us.

I wish I could have told them that I was scared
of the avocado bathroom and the statement floral kitchen tiles.

And the way the pine trees edged the garden
and we lost all our paper planes.

I didn't mean to hurt my brother,
but it was the kind of place that provoked murder.

Nothing around us for miles.
Just me and him too small to play with.

At least his teeth grew back.
When we left, I swear, there were eyes in the trees, watching.

Llangrannog Flatfish

And God saw everything that he had made, and, behold, it was very good.
Genesis 1:31

Father reeled it out of the sea like a miracle, the old oddity,
periscope eyes, spotted brown, so juicy it sizzled.
A family size fish, flattened, frilly as a doily.

I looked at it and wondered how something so ugly
could be very good. Splayed, with all of its peculiar abilities.
Not slick and quick, but lazy and lurking, still thick enough to get caught.

He coshed it to stop it gasping and he had dominion.
A million, billion years shuddered, stopped.
We thought of how to eat it, butter greased and fried.

Later, paws in the surf, a diabolic slobbering:
a Golden Retriever and its slack jaws
already halfway up the beach, chewing.

You bloody shitty creature! Nature in the raw,
the first time you swore.

The Elvis Rock

On the A44 there's a rock that says *Elvis*.
Whenever we pass it Father tuts. *Vandalism.*

He died last week, and next door played his records all day,
top volume. There were stories about a wooden heart
so ballooned and bloated, it exploded.

When I fall asleep, I see Elvis in his jumpsuit
singing *Love Me Tender* to the sheep.
Apparently, once, he was spotted down this way:

I was driving a Ford Anglia 105e.
As I drew close the guy on the left looked over his shoulder.
I immediately said to my wife 'That's Elvis!'
She did not disagree.

Later, one of our congregation paints *Jesus*
for a stunt. It will last less than a month.

Flower Festival

Women of the parish, lilies of the field, spun
out of the mossy damp, vases in thick windows.
All the Ruths, quietly bent over the business of display,
a life in murmurings over arrangements of apples and corn.

They spend all morning snipping, clipping stems
measuring radials, perfecting height and weight,
while I play with chips of green oasis
sweep with the cuttings of soft fern.

Mrs Byrne-Davies arrives with a bushel of bloated
lilies and carnations ordered from Carmarthen.
Dim byd ffanci, she breathes, *peth bach i'r ficer.*
The temperature of the church rises.

But her blowsy effort is too much for Mother
who doesn't speak the language,
and she wilts like someone clipped her stem.
This, after all, is what God thinks women are good for.

Mothers Union and Thinking of the Children,
and Flowers and Bara Brith and Harvest Festival.
Beneath the surface, when he's not looking,
they know it's war.

Next Door's Ford Cortina

From the bedroom window, we disapprove
of cousins, brothers, sons: heathens.
Welsh as the hills, whole families on the council,
a village of them, sprawled around the houses next door.
Cans of Double Diamond, packs of Players Number 6.
Big Daddy, Boss Hog on the overgrown lanes
taking sloppy corners, the spill of summer scratching his paintwork.

Every Sunday we troop off to church in our Sunday best,
while he polishes his jalopy. *Jesus Saves*, we tell him
primly as we pass. He grunts a bleary *Iechyd Da*.
He knows where he is going and never mind.

Hiding Place

The high wind whines through the cracks as if The Devil
Himself is trying to blow the house down, a heavy huff
and puff, and the windows might at any moment shatter.

Riding on the storm are figures from the book
of Revelation, in all their hysteric glamour,
throwing bitter rain at the glass, demanding to be let in.

Quick! My toys, piled against the windows, need saving
from the horsemen of the apocalypse and the seven beasts
with the faces of a leopard and the feet of a bear.

Scooping them in armfuls I push them beneath
the bedclothes. Ragdolly Anne and my favourite, little blue lamb,
anxious, snuffling, I wedge myself in there too, face first.

It soon gets hot and airless, but at least we are safe
from harm. Here, I learn the early principles of denial:
that what I cannot see, cannot be real.

Bodnant Gardens

The broadwalks stretch across the water like squares of hopscotch.
In the day's shimmer they seem to float above a body dark and full of weeds.

My replication, refracted, goes on and on, calling like an echo
across these vacant ponds and their shallow lilies.

Mother thinks it's beautiful, but I am full of vertigo,
as if I could fall at any moment, into the sky, which is not the sky.

I am confused by this landscape. I do not know which way is up
or how to walk on water. The surface is so far down.

Jubilee

Mother takes us to Carmarthen to see the Queen.
I'm in my Swiss National costume sent me by my aunt
who lives in Geneva, with another woman — though
we never talk about that. I am in love with Heidi,
and the mountains and all the cheese and sleeping
in a hayloft, though Mother says it would be prickly.

We wait for ages in the sun for her to come,
eating crisps and getting itchy. I need a wee but
Mother doesn't want to lose our spot. *Hold it in*
she says, which could be the story of her life.

Finally they appear, but it's a lottery which side,
and like always, we are on the wrong one.
We wave our flags valiantly, but we don't really want
Prince Philip, who trudges past muttering to himself,
eyes like a shied horse. She's across the road
in her pastel suit. We cheer but she does not turn.

When we get home, Father is reading the newspaper.
Punks are making an alternative celebration.
There is a terrible darkness taking over this country, he says.
I wonder what Heidi would do.

Beached Whale, Pendine Sands

Barnacled, slumped into the land, a vehicle to nowhere,
lapped, and stricken by seagulls, crabs, all the sharp,
articulated creatures.

Smelly, blubberish, shapeless as jelly,
with one kind eye closed,
lines folded as if into sleep.

Jonah was swallowed by it. That's all I can think
as I walk around its immensity. One gulp
and he was in the belly, easily

big enough to accommodate me.
But I wonder how he lived. At such
submarine depths, how he breathed,

inside the sticky void of that dark
cathedral. The fishy reek,
grazed by the rough rasp of tongue.

But we are not encouraged to ask such
practical questions. God is *mysterious* and *beyond
our understanding*, and that's all you need to know.

The stillness bothers me. The gaseous rot
and the surrender. Sea-lapped, lifeless and stinking.
Miracles are a far stretch from here.

Duw, Duw

Thou shalt not take the name of the LORD thy God in vain.
Exodus 20:7

People are so sinful here they say it twice, like a charm.
Or even thrice, especially if it's something shocking.
It means something like *well, well,* because saying *god, god*
after everything would actually be a bit hysterical.
I have learned that it's not the same as *cer i grafu!*
which you would only say if you wanted someone to scratch
their *anws blewog,* but I digress.
It came back to us, recently, that one of the sons
told the old man at the bar over beer,
that the vicar went to visit the hippies:

and this woman, see, opens the door of her van,
nude as the day she was born, and the vicar says:
aren't you going to put something on?
And she shrugs, then goes back in,
and comes back wearing her wellington boots!
Just like that. Swear on my mother's life.
And I asked the vicar, well what did you do?
Must have been difficult to tell her about Jesus,
under the circumstances.
And he says, well I'd say so, wouldn't you?
Of course I would boyo, duw, duw.

Cadair Idris

Up, hup, up! I trudge, in daps and flares and purple T-shirt.
Carrying my magic pillowcase with the fake Disney drawings,
magic, because like Aladdin's carpet
it enables me to navigate between sleep and wake.
Which is the most exciting part of my short life to date.

Today, we are soldiers, grown-ups,
heading for the summit, following my father's strides.
This the seat of Idris the giant. Who strode about
these parts with his heavy club and axes,
being generally scary.

I am overcome by a desire for the top
so intense it surprises me, in spite of blisters
I want to carry on along the ridge, scrambling
across scree to get there, where people fly flags
and leave tags and sign their names in a little black book.

Curious, and not for the first time, (and this will be the story
of my life). When we reach it I think even Father is impressed.
I fly the pillowcase, triumphant. Badly-drawn Dumbo
looks demented. We drink Bovril from a flask.
I lose the pillowcase on the long way back down.

Tracey's Party

I am running around with Tracey and her sisters.
They live three doors down, with the heathens,
but inexplicably I am allowed to go. I am jealous
she got an Etch-a-Sketch and a Flintstones Rotadraw,
and a Barbie that later we flushed down the loo.

She is my best friend. We have secrets and play
nicely, like the older sister I wish I had.
Back home something bad has happened.
And I don't know what Mother meant
when she said a miscarriage was not a typing mistake.

Retreat, The Hookses, Pembrokeshire

Men are considering what will happen at the end of time
while I play in the scruffs of gorse in the garden.
And the choughs with their red feet
fluff around the cliffs like demons.

People here spend a lot of time praying.
They have divined that at the end of days
when Jesus saves, all the unbelievers
will simply disappear. Dematerialise. Expire.

At the bottom of the cliffs the sea churns
blue and white, I lie on my belly and look down,
and wonder at the science of last things,
and the many ways we might die.

Annihilation: like turning off a television.
A dead light that sucks everything back
to its black heart. Heaven beyond is nice,
and full of us, being quiet.

Phyllis Baked Beans

In the morning, she stands in socks and sandals,
salt and pepper in her Edward the Confessor hair.
Stirring, with her strong right arm, round
and round for Jesus. Something is not right, if she could only put
her finger on it. In the shape of her husband's beard,
or the way the room is suddenly shrunk to the brassy
turning of the spoon. The badge that reads
Smile! God Loves You! wobbles as she stirs.

Rosacea flares across her cheeks, like the traces
of a firework, and what she wants, what she wants,
must never be spoken. Stripes of sunlight burn
across the window, and the yew tree's branches
snap like a whip. A spilled bean
bursts beneath the heavy bottom of the pan.

Black Sheep

We kept him in a pen by the vegetable patch,
fed him a bottle's teat through the chicken wire.
Not knowing any better, we called him Sambo,
and we loved him, in the way that we were taught to love
all mute things – fiercely for a while, and then resentfully
because he could not tell us about his suffering.

Defiantly, he grew larger, refused to be cute,
escaped into the garden and ate my mother's roses,
was found stopping traffic down the lane,
pulling up flowerbeds with his teeth. We hated him,
because now he was moronic, sheep:
some strange part of us, too big to pet.

The farmer came to get him, and said he was mutton now.
We didn't mind. On Sundays we ate lamb.

Llanymawddwy

It was an act so surprising that had I not witnessed it.
I could have thought it was a dream.

The Welsh pony had a skewbald mountain
roughness, chiselled from the land itself,
used to trekking up and down hills in search of lost sheep.
Mother mounted it as if it was something she did in her sleep,
rather than standing up front with Father, being wife.

John gave her the reins and she took off,
clip clopping up the lane, the backside of the animal
swinging like a roué and nevermind
all the accidents. I watched and wondered
if she would ever come back
to the cucumber sandwiches, the boiling tea urn.

Corona Pop Van

I'm playing with Nicola on the beanbag, while mother sews.
Drinking cherryade so bright it could be blood.
Whatever we are doing involves wrestling.

Giggling, tickling, strung out on jelly tots and tartrazine
close enough to kiss, her breath in my ear.
Outside the delivery van is stuck in the lane.

Gears grind like a friction burn. Mother is shocked.
Oh. Julia, no! Girls don't play like that! We sit up,
breathing hard, not sure what we did wrong.
Let's get fizzical, the truck ad says, riffing on the song.

Pickfords

The lorries are loaded like a rebuke
to all the godless of this parish.
We're moving on. Well, back, but still upwards,
to better things. A bigger house. A better church.
A revival that will sweep across this land.

Meanwhile, I am nine and weeping in my bedroom,
for all the things I forgot to pack,
and what I will never get back.

ABERAERON PART 2
(1980–1988)

Aberaeron Vicarage

Father stands on the doorstep in his cassock, surveying his new territory.
An acre, within sniffing distance of the salt-slowed sea.
With empty stables and an infestation of knotweed
that Mother calls the Burma Road. Rhododendron, and a noisy
blue-black rookery and a vegetable patch he'll soon turf over.

In the kitchen, a solid fuel Aga which will char the Pascal lamb
to ruin while the Christmas turkey stays pink after hours
of lukewarm digestion. The chipped enamel, the burnt flat of the hotplate,
the temperature dial flicking between here and nowhere, like
the controls of a plane falling out of the sky.

I'm not sure I like this house. There is no central heating
and the mahogany fireplace in the dining room rises to the ceiling.
A dust catcher with gothic tendencies and, instead of a fire, dusty electric
bars to warm the clergy who fall asleep over our china
with a sneaky nip of whisky in their tea.

In the other lounge there's an untuned piano that all three of us
will learn to play, clumsily thumping hymns
in the hope that we might turn out musical.
But in the choir they will ask me to sing quietly.
Already I know my short fingers have the finesse of livestock.

I have the room at the back that looks out over town, the garage,
the new housing estate, fields of sheep and, at a squint, the sea.
Below, is Father's study, the engine of this house,
centre of all correction, sermons, intercessions,
and his job, that sits on all our shoulders like a fog.

Upstairs, the bathroom where I will have my first orgasm,
and the playroom where Mother has a whole room for sewing,
and where I will undertake many serious school projects and my brother and I
will play wargames with his action men and hunt whales and imagine ourselves
elsewhere from this heavy house and its solemn furniture.

Parish News

And here is the news, cranked out with irritable irregularity
on an ancient Roneo, the black click whirr of the drum,
cogs marching to the onward beat of soldiers.

Every three pages is a blank, or disfigured
by spreading ink clots, blots, pages pleated into ladders
as if the machine is annoyed with itself
for broadcasting frowsty tracts and prayers.
I sort them into piles on the floor of Father's study,
chafing my knees on the cheap carpet tiles.

Hear ye, you wayward, stubborn, flock,
Here is the Good News: Vicar Bell Saves
and you heard it here first, in *Newyddion Y Plwyf.*

Disco Dancing Aberarth

It's late now and the music's pumping
all the children up and jumping
Abba and Cliff Richard thumping
and we're disco, disco dancing Aberarth.

She flares the hem of her skirt, and steps
inside the rhythm, in the dress sewed
by her mother. The task to be the last
one dancing and win a prize.

She twirls like the girl in *The Red Shoes*,
spins the ties of her skirt like a boudoir
accessory, not sure where she learned that move,
her arms swinging as if she is grasping

for something she will never quite reach.
For a second she feels almost beautiful
remembering to let her light shine.
Until she notices something unspoken

between the men, and her rivals begin
to lose, until she, the new vicar's daughter
is winning the colouring book and felt pens, and her father
laughs so hard at a joke no one else understands.

It's late now and the music's pumping
all the children up and jumping
Abba and Cliff Richard thumping
and we're disco, disco dancing Aberarth.

Urdd Gobaith Cymru

I am in Llangrannog doing adventurous things in Welsh
Mistair Urdd, Mistair Urdd, in your red, white, and green,
We are the hope of Wales.
I mumble whatever I don't understand.

More terrifying than Mistair Urdd with his stick arms and legs,
is The Black Nun. It says so in pencil and felt pen.
She haunts the bunk beds so hard that Nia will only sleep with the light on,
the bulb sizzling inches from my face. All night there is screaming.

We are learning *Nofio* in the green swimming pool, and later *Marchogaeth.*
Skills for confident, athletic girls who know where they come from
and where they belong. Not me on my dumpy pony bumping
around the ring so slowly that—

What happens next is speed, raw fear. A tense of flank,
yanking for the door, a spooked rebellion, equine fright,
raw fear. I'm barely hanging on. At some point we overtake a van.
Every bone in my body tensed to break,

every muscle moving the wrong way,
and the brawn and sweat and terrible awareness
that our whole family has bad luck with horses.
Then—ground at close range. Ringing in my ears.

I am dizzy. I have a temperature of 103.
The teachers call my parents and give me a cup of tea,
looking anxious. I will be bruised for a long while after.
They talk among themselves and make arrangements.

I wish I had known then that this is how life will feel:
a slipshod beast with careless reins and baggy tack,
galloping somewhere just beyond sight
with me on the back, practising directionality.

Winter 1982

The snow lies round in eight-foot drifts,
and an ancient wolf wind howls.
Bread is dropped by helicopter to the sports field.
We are cut off for a week.
Frost forms inside my bedroom window, patterns of ice
that I scratch at with my fingernails.

We walk at the level of the hedgerows. Through dips and troughs
where we can see the roofs of cars. The scalding air thickens
our breath. My brother loses his boot.
When we get home we are shivering and have no electricity.
In this huge new house, every room is cold.

Father stokes the fire and we sit with our feet,
socks steaming, inside the pan warmer.
Like Shadrach, Meshach and Abednego
we walk through tongues of fire, righteous,
hotter still and hotter, and yet we are not consumed.

The Sisters

Brown habits and pruned faces. Sitting in the best room,
on heavy floral armchairs. I stare at them.
They stare at me. I do not know what to say.
They are not unkind. They live in a place far away

and do good works. They wear thick crosses and sit
so tidy they could be statues. But still they scare me.
The austerity. Nothing except what is received.
Everything measured into units of correction.

Do you live in a house?
We do.

Is it like our house?
It's bigger.

Do you have your own rooms?
Of course.

Are you married?
To Jesus, yes.

When they are gone, I lie awake for hours, afraid,
that God wants me, is calling me to evensong
in long corridors, whitewashed walls,
bread like stone – so still everything screams.

Special Needs

I'm fat and this has become a problem.
Both for me, and for my mother who is
often on a diet.
We have free school dinners,
mostly variations on carbohydrate.
And it has been decided that it is this
that is making me chubby.

I am a new girl on a new table
with the wheelchairs and the allergics.
One of them needs help to eat.
I have in front of me
two long lettuce leaves instead of chips.
Not for the first time, I wish I were
Catholic and I could pray to saints.

The People's Princess

Princess Diana is getting married and everyone
is going on about her frock.
We go round to Jackie's house
because they have a colour TV to watch.

We get free mugs at school, and commemorative coins.
We don't ask questions then. Royalty is what we do,
which is somehow connected to how we feel,
but this cannot be articulated yet.

She walks up the aisle like statuary being wheeled to its station,
chiselled for all millennia with her beseeching expression
and frozen princess face. And her eyes. Her eyes!
Charles, the stiff in the suit who slots her into place.

The golden trumpets sound in the cathedral,
and subject to such majesty, and the syrup
of the commentary, we are subdued.
The grown-ups coo and sip champagne.

Later, we play kissing games in the garden,
heads full of baroque symmetry and the tether
of that dress. We take turns to be Charles and Di,
not yet sure whose side we're on.

Hair Curlers

Mother has a new contraption, part sci fi, part fetish gear
which allows her to set her perm while she does the ironing.

The motor sits across her shoulder like a handbag,
and she wears a hood puffed up in a latex cloud.
She looks alien, modern, and somehow sexual.

I don't know why I want to know it,
or why I want to know it now,
but I have a very important question:
Mum, what's a lesbian?

Being Tarzan

We are on a walk a long way from town,
immersed in the forest, the kind of straight
managed trees that strike like matchsticks,
or torches. Of course I want to be Tarzan,
and force my brother to be Jane.

The ground smells of wet pine, Welsh soil.
In my mind I swing from vines, leap
from stone to stone, landing like a pro. Instead
there is my sad balance, my myopia, my lack of clearance.
A branch pierces and rips across my groin.

My bombproof Terylene trousers remain intact.
Oh come on what's up? she says, *trust you
to fall off a log.* But I am winded and cannot move.
It hurts.
She looks at me. *Nothing wrong with you.*

What she cannot see, is the eight-inch gash,
just to the right of what I have no word for.
When, eventually she looks she nearly faints.
There is skin and blood and white stuff
the same colour as her face.

Later in the hospital they stitch me up, muttering
about luck, *another centimetre and who knows
what could have happened.* Mother is revived
by hot chocolate and all the fuss, while I lie there
staring at the ceiling, practising not feeling.

School Sports

I'm secondary now. Different uniform, different
part of town. Comprehensive.

I have started bleeding, a mysterious event
which Father blessed me for, although I didn't understand it.

I am aware that this is God's curse on Eve for being nosy.
Mother gives me a book with biological drawings.

She has also given me a sanitary pad, cannon wadding
which sits in my knickers like a medical emergency.

In the afternoon it's sports and Miss Parry makes us run
around the track. While I'm lumbering something comes

unstuck. It pokes from my shorts like a dead duck tail,
my ignorance, my shame, my typical bad luck.

Greenham Common

We do a drive-by around the chain link fence,
which is full of fabric, rubbish, scraps of tents, slogans:
Nuclear Weapons No Thanks.
There are women chained to it with cropped hair and mannish clothes
and pictures on the news of lesbians holding hands.
Look kids, living history, Mother says. Inside me, something quivers.

One of the protestors said on telly that the world is run by mad old men.
It's hard to disagree. Especially when there are starving children.
Father tuts at all the squalor, only ever tourists
hiding on our cloud, in the world but not of it.
And if we're honest, we cherish anything that hastens the apocalypse.
Our life is not really here, but at the end of days. We are prepared.

Four Fathers

I'm supposed to be getting married to Jesus or something
but frankly, it doesn't make much sense, and I'm far more
interested in why Megan's sister said I was a lemon at school.
Here I am, head bowed, presided over by bishop so and so.
All around me the heavy sweet of churches and the syrup
of communion wine and death, so much bloody death.

Just think of all that suffering. The torture of that death,
the one death, the true death, the only death. It's all about death,
you'll see. Because I forgot to tell you: you're going to die.

In our family, there are two dead fathers: the first a pilot
who feared not, did loop the loops for breakfast
pulled out of nosedives just for fun,
and exploded like a firework in a field of forever England
when my mother was barely born.

The other, a soldier with a lingering, sickly, bedside grim,
the kind that festers, drives people mad,
part of the man who is cassocked in my father.
Here on confirmation day, they haunt me:
the grandfathers that I never had.

And the consequence is here: me in Sunday best,
trapped inside a double negative, trying to feel blessed.

Billy Graham Crusade, 1984

The stadium is stuffed singing, there are tambourines.
Everyone is swaying in their outdoor coats.
I think it rained.

He is so small, down there on the podium, but
his voice carries down the ages, with its
booming oration.

Like all the best salesmen he has a time limited offer.
Hear me now, and be changed for ever, or ignore me
and move on, but remember –

here he thumps his Bible, the old pro –
the wages of sin are death.
Sin. The word itself a curse,

so easy to fall in. Later, he does an altar call,
invites the gathered to submit
to his charisma.

Father copies him. We have services where
he says the same things about making a decision,
as if he is selling a special offer television.

People jump the barriers, sprint,
we are witnessing phenomena,
as natural as an eclipse.

Kings Hall, Aberystwyth

Den of iniquity is what she calls it, and I am dying to go in.
Drooling with a milkshake at the Milk Bar
after another session at the dentist fixing my wayward teeth.
I stare at shocking pink walls and rusting ironwork.

Aberystwyth is much bigger than Aberaeron,
fizzier, tackier, a source of much suspicion.
Full of Brummies and outsiders
come for the University. And all of the iniquity.

The basement arcade with its dodgems
and shove pennies and blinking fruit machines
and candyfloss and fights and the big sea that throws
its stones at the bandstand and the awkward promenade.

Led Zeppelin played 'Stairway to Heaven'
and a medley of 'Whole Lotta Love',
it seems like the best place ever to be a bored
thirteen-year-old. One day we will move here

which I will find surprising, considering how much
Mother disapproves. When they tell me, I am thrilled,
finally, somewhere with the opportunity for cheap wickedness.
But by the time we get there, it will have closed.

French Exchange

Of course we go to Brest.
The only kind of foreign suitable
for a preacher's daughter.

Je m'appelle Julia, *comment allez vouz?*
I slide my tongue inside the language
thinking it will make me cool,

like red wine and cigarettes.
Here, there are supermarkets big as sheds,
Nutella, Gauloises, a whiff of sex,

the vinegar of table wine. Old ladies show
their lace, cheese smells of feet,
and there are snails.

In the French house, with the French
people, it is foggy with Gitanes
and the dark of the French father

who, after fighting with his wife,
cuts the lawn in a thunderstorm.
I watch him from the bedroom window,

churning grass to silage,
swearing blue *merde*, electricity
simmering in the foreign air.

In the morning,
I have my ears pierced
in the market in Quimper.

Two golden studs gleam
all the way home.
My Jezebel ears, my souvenir.

The Study

Questioning, is what he calls it.
Or seeking. These are the people
who come for lingering conversations
that turn his tea cold. They are interested
in coming over to our side

but it involves a lot of prayer
and talking. So much talking.
This is how people see the light,
all of them who live in the darkness
outside this house.

Especially the divorcees.
I often wonder what goes on in there
when his secretary has gone home.
And there are just the two chairs
around the electric fire.

Where do they come from?
Especially at mealtimes.
Especially when Mother
is just outside the door,
fist raised to knock.

Milk Snatcher

Father thinks she's great. He tells us so at tea.
He enjoys the nightly news where rabbles
of dirty miners have it handed to them.
These Marxists with their utopias need to get real.

She is bringing back stability, certainty,
to a hairy country, old and badly clothed,
with naïve teeth and a childish sense of
pageantry. She is telling us

who we are again. And even those
most disinclined to listen to a woman,
love her matronly, no nonsense ways,
and the righteousness of her hair.

Jesus said we should love the poor,
not tut at them on the news.
I will live long enough to know
I am witnessing the slow death of South Wales.

I have started blushing when I get upset, and at the tea table
wear my NUM badge, sent by the miners. Father
thinks it's the funniest thing he's ever seen.
I wrote to them after the news. My cheeks are on fire.

May's Funeral

We go back to Llangeler for the funeral.
Father does not come, because the new vicar
disapproves of our evangelical ways.
Just me and Mother, and the kind of day

that sours faith, lived in the haze of a sudden
heatwave. We, sweating inside the damp
limewash with the casket up the front
breasted by a single bunch of lilies.

In the family pew he rocked himself, calling
like a blind kitten, *Mam, Mam.*
You could smell the straightjacket on him,
all that weeping, indecent on a man.

At the graveside he took up an axe,
and stirred it about the clouds,
then brought it against the coffin
as if he could split apart death,

and bring her back to the living
in her housecoat and tans,
taking in the warming doorstep milk,
waving life to the delivery van.

Snapdragons

So nice to see you've got your mother visiting, Vicar Bell.
That's what the lady of the parish said. Trying so hard
to curry favour that I could practically smell it cooking.

My mother is grubbing in the flower beds,
in her house coat and slippers, being private.
I am following her around

playing with the Antirrhinums making dragon faces
snap open and shut. *Mistook me for his mother …*
I suppose I could do more with my hair, but with you three and the parish

and anyway it's terribly difficult to eat only 800 calories a day
when you're feeding the five thousand. What can I do?
The dragon mouths want to ask why it matters,

but moving only laterally, they are limited in their
capacity for articulation, instead they look shocked
when she says, *I don't want him to leave me.*

Mary and Martha

*But Martha was cumbered about much serving, and came to him, and said, Lord,
dost thou not care that my sister hath left me to serve alone?* Luke 10:40

Typical. The minute there's a man about the house
she's off, leaving me to get on
with the gutting of fish, the buttering of bread.
Sitting there, simpering, playing with her
beads in that idle, flirty way that makes her look cheap.

Five loaves and fishes and then some
piled on the table, there's at least fifty people coming,
it will take a miracle to get this done in time.
And all she cares about is boys, boys, boys,
turned into a simpleton the minute they arrived.

Our hands butterflied across the table,
slicing, dicing, picking bones, tossing salads,
while we debated the various defences of Kierkegaard,
and the finer points of the theories of mind,
and then when he arrived she emptied like a drain.

Quite the coquette, while I sit here steaming
Pollack, getting grease stains on my blouse.
So many exceptions: Peter who's vegetarian, Matthew
the wheat intolerant, Mark who can't stand fish.
Wet drips together dripping. Especially *him*.

When I went out to complain all he could say
was there were more important things than cooking
in that kind of hippie, dreamy way that she believes
is a substitute for thinking. See here, he said,
picking a flower, consider the lilies of the field.

And she lay next to him, giggling, rococo,
as if posing for a Titian. God, that made me mad.
Here I am up to my eyeballs in dishes,
and all she can think about is sex. What good are flowers
when the clock is ticking on the Sunday roast?

He's no idea what it's like to be pulled
every which way, clean this, cook that, where's my
clean shirt? He might have time for stargazing,
but me, I have to keep the carrots from boiling over.
A martyr? Don't be soft. I'm losing my mind in here.

M.E.

Mother has taken to her bed.
Lying in a dark room with the curtains shut.

I make the tea, put the laundry on.
Wonder at what led to her condition.

She has always been prone to being sickly,
but this is a different sort of malady.

Her symptoms are a Victorian mystery.
She is whey-faced, mystic.

The doctors think she is procrastinating.
On the news, they call it malingerers entropy.

She goes the homeopathic route.
Swallows white herbs and old wives' tales.

But this fatigue will blink on and off for years,
a fizzing lightbulb on a low current.

I feel as if I'm in a kind of training.
What can I do but watch and pray?

Room Five

A whole generation of Welsh
will learn the history of English
Literature in this green room. All the greats:
Austen, Shakespeare, Byron, Keats.

Here is our new teacher, with her sharp
Joan Collins glamour and good Welsh accent,
whose approval, is suddenly, inexplicably,
embarrassingly, crucial to my survival.

Language becomes a thing I do
for her, words fly from my pen like prayers.
Here, I will blush my way through five years of school,
turning pages one heartbeat at a time.

Gentleman of the Road

He emerged from the hedgerow as if from the Bible, Methuselah
of the fields, stinking like six weeks of rubbish left out in the sun,
his coat a strayed flap of mac hanging in ribbons around his beard.

One of those, Mother mouthed with a groan, as she portioned out
supper, even though all the homeless are prophets in disguise.
I watch him, sat on the back step, loose limbed, the bones

in his face showing like death, and I imagine him like John the Baptist
in the wilderness, thrusting an arm inside the belly of a tree, up to his shoulder,
feeling about blind, pulling out the comb, full of sun and the rich hum of locusts.

He leaves soon after, plate abandoned by the stairs. That night I go to bed,
unfed, thinking of Salome, and his head on a platter, and although
he cannot speak, two lips lick – pink – inside the grey tangle of his face.

Like Turkeys for Christmas

We kept them in the stables and they grew
like slow balloons. Made bizarre noises, a kind
of swallowed *Duw, Duw*, as if they couldn't open their
beaks wide enough to talk so they ventriloquised.

We looked after these ones the best;
they had a higher purpose than to be pets.
We fed them good grain and kitchen scraps,
watched them getting fatter.

Until they are the size of large children,
and we begin to dread Christmas.
1. *Make sure your knives are sharp.*
2. *Hold the turkey by its feet.*

3. *Put it in the killing cone.*
4. *Cut the artery and let it drain.*
Father goes a funny
colour when he reads this bit.

In the end, we have to get the woman
from the farm. I stand outside
listening: a snow of feathers swirling,
a wordless white deadening.

The Other Vicar's Daughter

There is a family with a caravan parked on our front lawn.
Another vicar on holiday, saving money on site fees.
They have a daughter, older than me, only a few months,
but in the mediation of teenage time, Jurassic.
Also, they are from England.

At her insistence we play loud, unfamiliar games, with rules
I don't understand. Someone slams my finger in the door.
She is pure vicar's daughter, pure will, feral in her competition.
I don't even know what we are competing for. Except, suddenly,
I lose my temper, and the atmosphere of the vicarage chills.

I try to turn my back, serious, bigger, I have books to read.
But this makes her even more annoyed.
She comes into my room, listens to my music,
rearranges all my Sindy dolls into submissive positions
while telling me how she prays ten times a day.

When they leave I take a shower. There are creatures
drowning in the soapy water and everyone is itchy.
Penitently, we comb our hair. Holding jelly
eggs to the light, I ask my mother what they are.
She bites her lip. *Parasites*, she replies.

Pilchard Sandwiches

It's a complicated situation. Grandmothers who don't match.
One on each side, widows most of their lives,
one big, one small.
The big one is maternal, posh, big houses
and big gardens, stomach of Empire.

The other side is feral. Little but not small.
All knuckles, street fighter, back biter,
superstitious, suspicious, full of pub lore,
one of ten who swept rooms and cleaned out
spittoons, a pub rat who lived on her guts.

With Mother being ill someone else needs to look
after me. I am fifteen, and staying with the big one
in the Devon countryside which is like being on vacation
in a vat of lard with extra cream on everything.
We have spent a week eating and watching TV.

And I have read nearly all of *Lady Chatterley's Lover*
although I became confused when twenty pages
seemed to have been removed. She is a Quaker which
means we go to a silent service which is much better
than all that talk of Jesus as your best friend.

Now I must go home. I am meeting the little one
on the train from Torquay.
The sketchy side of the English Riviera.
Daily Mail and Royal biscuit tins, bridge nights
and a two-bar electric fire.

We sit opposite each other in the swaying
carriage. She still has a pipe cleaner
that she uses to curl her hair.
When it falls out she laughs and twirls
it in a dangerous spiral around her finger.

But it's when she gets the sandwiches out
that everything kicks off. I am already full,
with cereal and croissants and Devon air.
A fishy smelling sandwich is the last
thing I have the stomach for.

But refusal is a very bad idea.
She tells the ladies sitting next to us,
how she got up at five am and I am an ungrateful
granddaughter for not eating her carefully prepared
mashed tinned pilchards on two-day-old bread.

Perhaps it's the poverty of her offering that makes
her angry. Something in her knows she is not
as classy as my other granny, will never know
which knife and fork to use and will always put
sweetened condensed milk in her tea.

But she will not be silenced by politeness,
and if I want to know where I get it from
I do not need to look any further than this gene pool,
nothing makes us crazier than feeling ignored.
Until she stands up, luggage and all.

I'm going back. Where I'll be respected.
Never in all my born days … And so on and on.
I am frenzied with apology.
But it's like trying to capture mercury,
she keeps finding another level of attack.

At Bristol Parkway she leaves me on the platform,
leaves me to get the train to Wales alone.
I am at a loss for language. How to explain
that to something as simple as a sandwich I lost my grandma?
Already I know I will be infamous in family lore.

The train pulls out and I rattle on towards Wales
looking out the window unsure of what will happen next
until I see her, coming down the aisle, searching for a seat,
as if nothing at all were ever out of place.
She even lifts a hand to wave.

Weight Watchers

What can you say that would make sense
to anyone who does not live in your house?
Your body has become detached from itself,
and sprouts at all the wrong angles,
always in the wrong clothes.
Pink dresses and long socks,
a perversity of adolescence, amplified.

You are not being bred for the background.
You must be looked at, but not adored.
Be not fat, but be not beautiful either,
because vanity distracts,
and so quickly tips over into sluttishness,
painted nails and earrings,
and the terrible prospect of sex.

You are here because you are not quite
doing something right and you are not yourself.
But you are not sure what you are becoming either.
With these heavy Welsh women huffing
against age and butter and their own
bitterness at the weighing scales.
Success and failure measured in teaspoons.

You feel your body like a balloon, or an enclosure,
too pink, too flashy. Flesh. The word is like a leash.
Cnawd. It gnaws. It must be contained.
Especially if it belongs to you, especially if it shows.
Sin, rolling from the top of your jeans.
Discipline, that's what you need. Inexplicable then,
that for the third week running, you have gained.

Centre for Alternative Technology

They are so hippie they have a compost toilet
that traumatises all of us.

All the way round Father scoffs at the recyclable
displays on climate change and self-sufficiency.

He has dug beds and turned earth and allotments.
Fished, kept rabbits for food, known hardship.

This bunch of damp wool jumpers smelling of roll ups
and slacking, don't know their luck,

and he starts to witness to the guy selling tickets.
And what about your relationship with Jesus?

I always thought it was because we were holy that people
stared at us. Now I wonder what it is they see.

Dyke on a Bike

She comes to us on a Kawasaki ZX10,
its exoskeleton throbbing between her legs.
They have her in the study for hours
praying the gay away while the engine cools.
I run my sticky fingers across the sheen of its wheels,
the heat of the seat, wondering at what has brought her,
itinerant grease monkey, fingers smeared with oil,
to the garage across the road.

She wears a skirt for confirmation and full
immersion baptism, and my mother cries.
I thought there was something awkward about the way
the dress hung on her narrow, boyish frame.

Later, she runs off with the verger's wife.
They come to church, hold hands, and giggle up the back
before roaring off, triumphant, having found
the kind of love that they were looking for.

Chernobyl Dandelions

Our new curate is trendy and likes beer.
Mother, who thinks all alcoholic beverages
are from the devil, disapproves.

There has been a nuclear accident in the USSR.
I look at grey pictures on the news and wonder at lives
lived elsewhere and feel – briefly – lucky.

Then comes the rain, and the anxiety.
Everything is toxic, an invisible seepage,
blows on ill winds to our green and sodden land.

One day, the curate picks all the dandelions from our lawn,
adds them to the brew that sits in his kitchen window,
a brown sludge, quietly burping in its dusty demijohn.

After a month it stops, and grows green mould.
Radiation sickness, he says, pouring it down the drain.
Divine intervention, Mother replies. Important to know the difference.

Bedside Prayers

God grant Margaret a pomegranate
the poem of fruits, a praise of jewels
come to rest by this hospital bed
in her dying hours.

God grant Margaret a pomegranate
for she has been asking after Persephone
tricked by Hades to eat when starving,
the six seeds of the berried flesh.

God grant Margaret a pomegranate
because inside this seeded apple
is a heart, a beating hymnal,
blood against the tongue.

Diary of a Young Crusader: Tour of the Holy Land 1987

Day 1: Departure Gate

A cold coming we had of it, such a long journey
through the night from Wales to the cheapest car park at Gatwick,
and the ways dark and my mother's sandwiches
curdling in their tin foil.

I, who at fifteen, have been no further than France,
am suddenly jet-set, international. Filling in for my mother
on this guided tour. I navigate the shiny halls of airport commerce,
submit to being patted down. Unusually, I am too excited
to eat. I carry my mother's sandwiches
for my father. A ham and cheese defence
against anxiety which, being thrifty, we cannot bear to throw away.
By the time we reach Departures,
they are heavy as albatross.
I push them under a plastic bucket seat.
We board the plane.

This being The Holy Land, we are checked
and double-checked. I have a dim awareness
of the news, of hostages, of planes in foreign airports,
people shot. But this won't happen here,
on this Kosher airline with the Hassidim and the businessmen
and the singular Arab few, who look
as if they have had their pockets turned inside out.
We are late and getting later, the air conditioning whines.
Eventually, a stewardess returns, a pendulum of sandwiches
swinging from her finger. *These*, she says, looking slightly
weary, *have caused a bomb scare. Whose are these?*
I slide down in the seat next to my father who is
flicking through *The Church Times*.
We do not raise our hands.

Day 2: Onward Christian Soldiers

The souk swarms with the devout,
as the maqam of the muezzin in his minaret
calls out the Adhan: *there is no God but Allah,
Muhammad is the messenger of God.*

We are pressed between them like a string of washing:
Herod's Gate, Jerusalem, 1987. The shops sell olives,
oranges, mounds of seeded challah,
rugs, crosses, Hanukah candelabras, crescent moons.

It smells of loud men, a swarthy, unfamiliar
thickness, after the pale soap of Welsh skin
– a different kind of modesty – and of spices,
sweat, grease from the falafel stand, lamb.

An unseen hand cups my bum and squeezes.
Shocked, I scurry forwards through the maze
of narrow streets, but Father is too far up the front,
leading as if his life depended on it.

Day 3: Via Dolorosa

At a station of the cross I weave between the crowds
to find a pool of children, and from beneath their legs,
my father's trainers pointing to the sky. The man in the shop
selling sheepskins chases them away and lifts him up.

He looks like a figure from the olden times. *Here we are*, Father
said at breakfast, *living history, back inside the
pages of the Bible.* But in the shop, I can almost see
the cartoon stars, the twittering Tom and Jerry halo.

He is not quite himself. *Go away!* he shouts.
Bring me a mirror! He peels his lips to inspect
his chipped tooth, his unconscious stranger than he knew.
When the ambulance comes, we do not go too.

Day 4: The Western Wall

To get there we must pass between two girl
soldiers not much older than myself,
carrying machine guns. A shock. In the way
they stand aside to let us pass, something thrills.

HaKotel HaMa'aravi, Ḥā'iṭ Al-Burāq call it
what you will. The wall itself is burnished by foreheads,
and the cracks between the stone
are mortared with prayers. Here is the ear of God.

The orthodox nod their incantations,
*Pray here for forty days and you will meet your sweetheart,
your sick mother will rise from her bed and walk.*
Tourists mill about taking photos.

I cover my head and touch the surface,
shiny and pitted, the limestone of kings,
so heavy that even a bomb might not destroy them,
and I wonder to whom, or what, I should pray.

Day 5: Mrs Morgan on The Mount of Olives

The animal kneels before her, supplicant, soft,
then wobbles to a stand and lurches her aloft,
She squeals and the gold chain of her glasses
slaps against her cheeks while the rest of us watch.

She laughs, then steadied, surveys the scene:
Jerusalem, Gethsemane, and the Al Aqsa mosque.
She quotes a verse from Zachariah and then the book of Acts.
This is where Jesus went to heaven, and where, allegedly, he will come back.

For a moment she is golden, like the dome on the rock.
no one can see more than this Welsh woman in her beaded smock.
We look at her nicely because her husband died last year: tied an anchor
round his neck, and leapt, and we must suffer for those whom Jesus Saves.

Day 6: Fishers of Men

They have gone to Galilee to think about fishermen.
I lie in the white hotel floating on my own nausea,
hallucinating in front of the TV. They are showing *Dallas*.
Everyone goes on about it at school,
I think that watching it might make me trendy,
except that the picture swirls before my eyes
with Arabic subtitles, dubbed into Hebrew.

Every now and then I bob to the bathroom to throw up,
and the fabric of the world ripples as if I had put
my finger to the surface of a pond. I could almost believe
that I am underwater, swimming, waiting to be caught.
At one point JR Ewing has a fishhook in his cheek,
and I see my father dragging him off screen stage right.
On the bus they will be singing songs about the light.

Day 7: Hebron

Abraham and Isaac and Jacob lie here, and to a lesser
extent, the wives. The day has a hot kind of temper and
I lean against some antiquity or other ignoring the prayers.
In the centre of the old town under an ancient tree

they sit and wait for us. Spitting
husks into the dust, staring darkly at their sandals
while we troop off to look at the tombs.
In the distance, I watch them arguing with our guide.

What do I know, in my Peacocks blouse, of life in an
occupied country? We are shepherded to the gift shop
where I spend too much pocket money
on Christmas decorations, a dove of peace.

There are more of them now, maybe twenty, talking about us,
I can tell. As the bus turns, there is a tinny *thwock*
of stone hitting metal, then another, Mrs Morgan screams.
I look back, with their raised arms they are almost waving.

Room Five Reprise

I think the heat might have gone to my head.
I am seized by the terrible idea that my English
teacher might die and I would be in heaven,
obviously, without her. Devotion pools
like a swelling blood spot,
thickening at the tip of the finger.

I give her a leaflet, a Bible verse,
If my people shall humble themselves,
and pray. She takes it graciously.
Half aware that I am being perverse
I carry on. *Aren't you frightened?*
Of what might happen when you die?

Henfenyw Churchyard

He drives away, leaving me, fifteen, alone, afraid,
a car drawls past, but does not stop, a sense of dread
pervades. Pausing at the lychgate, I cross myself,
set my Walkman loud. My task to record
the names of all the folk that lie around.

The broken teeth of gravestones, lichen,
weeds, shaking poplars, the razor call of swallows,
ancient yew trees. Every now and then a posy,
a plastic rose, a visit by some relative, perhaps
an American, nostalgic for home.

Antique and listing: here's Doctor Pugh, the weathered
wives of Farmer Jones, Eliza Williams and all her children,
perished in a fire in 1872. Meadowed in the corner,
the unmarked plots – tinkers, vagrants, thieves –
where once was found a leather boot with a leg still lying inside.

By lunchtime, I am bored and Paul Simon palls,
the sun is hot, the day is blue, around me life calls:
the chemistry of summer, the fizzing heat of bees.
I try the door but the church is locked, a sulk of stone
and glass, last week's service sheet chopping in the breeze.

I sit on Ebenezer Williams, drink a can of pop,
suck a humbug and wonder at the congregation
that worship at this lost and lonely spot.
Afterwards, my sugared blood runs high in the long grass,
and dancing, I lift up my top – see ye my tits you dead – *I'm alive*.

Haworth

Dear Charlotte,

You won't believe it but, my father has swapped
with the vicar and now we're staying up the road
since they turned the old one into a museum
on account of all your books.
Which I love, by the way.

We looked round and it smelled damp,
and those tombs so close to the house.
How did you live? Cooped up in there
the curtains shut, death seeping beneath the doors?
No wonder Emily went first.

I know how it feels: the undertaker
always knocks at teatime. Someone is always
having a disaster. Why do we all turn out to be
writers? Why does claustrophobic
repression provoke confession?

You will probably be unsurprised to learn
that the new vicarage is damp. There is a
machine in the basement that sucks out
all the water in the air, but you'd probably
be alarmed by such a contraption

given as how all you had was a fatty coal fire,
and candles to light your way.
I have felt your spirit moving through me.
And I'll try to be a good disciple, because,
tell me, it's important, am I not like you?

La Rochelle

We have spent the whole vacation like thieves,
looking for English number plates to push
a leaflet beneath the windscreen blades.
Our service is held in the Pine Circle on Sundays.
Even on holiday, especially on holiday,
there are people searching for the Lord.

We sleep in a creaky caravan where I practise
my schoolgirl French. I smoke Gauloises
in the showers and get sunburn. My brother
eats a dodgy prawn and my blonde sister
goes brown. Highlight of the holiday
is seeing Michelle from school in La Rochelle.

I have been witnessing to her for months.
Our letters to each other are of a devoted, Christian
kind, scrawled pictures of cats and verses
from the Bible. We sit on a bench our legs touching
and the world turns yellow and bright.

Suddenly, I am in a film of my life:
a French harbour with a Polaroid glare.
The rays of her hair catching the light,
dry lips dreaming of a kiss
the whole of that salted afternoon.

ABERYSTWYTH
(1988–1989)

Crossville Wales

Even though we have moved, I must return each morning
before the rest of the world is up,
make my way to the *Gorsaf* for the X96
that chunders its way to Aberaeron in a fog
of filthy black smog. The only buses for a thousand miles,
with no suspension, and smoking up the back.

I come to know the stops like the stations of the cross:
Llanrhystud Bridge, where Cochyn's dad drove his lorry
off the edge and drowned. The corner at Blaenplwyf,
where the milkman crashed his Mini, and we looked at the grey putty
of his body even though Mother told us not to.
Llanon, where someone pulled a knife at the cashier in VG.
Aberarth, where later one of my school friends will be murdered
in a slaying so gruesome it will make the national news.

In this suspended hour I learn to love
the lassitude of travel, the increments of difference
between this lamp post and that sign, every blade of grass
various depending on the time. This is my education:
classroom of the bus stop, lecture theatre of the sky,
the worsted bracken, the tapestry of fields, and the clouds
of change streaming thickly toward me across the mountains;
an angry pan left boiling on the stove.

Patrick

And so he comes. Scarves around his wrists, an Aerosmith headband
that he had blessed. The curly locks of a disciple and good
grooming of a celebrity: but with conditions.
Why should the Devil have all the best music? he asks.

He is Straight Edge. Metal for Jesus. He sings clean lyrics
while pulling rockgod crotch moves. It is certain he is confused.
By his body, I mean and Jesus, whom he obviously wants
to be, in an entirely sexual slash non-sexual, kind of way.

Cringing in the pew, it is clear I am in a different kind of church now.
Friendly, trendy, strange in its intensity. Later there will be tongues.

Gifts of the Spirit

It begins with a hum. Then arms
raised like branches, fingers stretched,
pushing back the sun or reeling it in.

All around human moaning, their eyes closed.
Such supplication to the roof, the sky.
Then comes the babbling. What *are* these tongues?

The verger burbles as if the organist
is playing him backwards. Father talks of
the nearness of God. His spirit moving among us.

The ambient cooing of the music group.
Mrs Morgan is moved to cry. I could be
reading, playing tennis, practising violin.

Instead, I close my eyes and squeeze.
The kind of clenching that forces
tears, or a fart.

Dark spots beneath my eyes,
a heartbeat against the light.
Is that God?

The Rainbow

They kiss in naked black and white,
grainy, on the tiny portable that I took
upstairs before the prayer meeting.
The aerial must be mangled to get a signal
and the picture is appalling, but it's enough
to provoke arousal in this attic evening.

Half mad with a kind of longing only Lawrence
has the words for, I stare at them embracing
in the water, the thrill of soft curves, touching.
Then someone pulls the plug. My mother, the colour of
communion wine. *God intended me to know,* she says.
Often, I think he wanted me to know too.

Signs and Wonders

They brought unto him many that were possessed with devils: and he cast out the
spirits with his word, and healed all that were sick.
Matthew 8:16

I cannot tell you what is going on round here except
a guttural screeching that fills the house with keening.
There are people in this church who believe
they are possessed by demons. Dark shadows
plague them, like characters from ancient oil paintings.
For them, the fabric of the world is so porous it leaks.

Coming from the front room is a sound so absurd
and terrible I think that someone is being murdered.
Though perhaps a murder victim might sound quieter,
being as how they would be dying and everything.
Mother shuts the kitchen door and turns the radio up
but it doesn't cover the disconcerted feeling.

Something happened to this lady somewhere foreign.
A missionary, she believes she has been cursed.
Maybe I'm just not that visionary, but I wonder
what it feels like to have two minds inside one body,
I try to move my teacup with my thoughts
but it just sits there, rebuking me, static.

Aberystwyth Castle

From my attic window I can see its listing ruin.
Thick stone walls that speak of other, rougher times,
beards and suits of armour. A craggy turret faces seawards
breasted, literally, by the war memorial: a bronze
woman, thick set, tits pointing out to sea,
hair chiselled by the tousled elements.

My grandmother laughs at this. She thinks it typical
of the hypocritical in men to give themselves
the opportunity to perve while pretending to be moral.
Even so, she admires that statue for a long time,
while we play hide and seek among the ruins,
even though I am too old for it now.

Across the car park is the church, rotting and impractical,
Its stones leach salt and the winter wind displaces tiles.
The smell of candle wax and brass polish, dust and carpets and
woodworm treatment. Of old ways and old thoughts.
Here I sing hymns, rattle a tambourine, hand out leaflets
in defence of life, though I am unsure how I was conceived.

And I wonder at the last person to leave the castle.
At what point was the rusting armour set aside?
When did they get tired of war? Were they longing
for a change of scene? To be done with the burden of everything,
to live in other, quieter, houses? To see another view,
not just rain pushing in from Ireland all the time?

Lee Abbey

I am at the Valley of the Rocks, surrounded by goats,
living in a strange house full of evangelicals.
Yesterday, an adder crossed my path and we prayed about
its meaning for an hour. I am on the Hobart rota, crawling on all fours,
right inside the guts of the industrial dishwashing machine.

I remember how it was. Blistered hands and Bible study.
Lots of sexual, non-sexual touching and post-work massage.
Or walks to Jenny's Leap to watch the sunset and wonder
at what Jenny leapt for. I fancy a South African butch called Fran
and go drinking with Matthew who is camp as tents.

We walk to Woody Bay in the dark and drink Bacardi and Coke
and feel rebellious. And smoke through our hangovers
and skip prayer meetings. We are what they call
backsliding, though it feels more exhilarating than that.
Often, I wonder what would happen if I just let go.

Oswestry

I get a taxi. The dark market town,
a half-timbered, in-between world,
on a freezing, foggy day. A place with a foot in Wales
and the other in some medieval English dream.

I am supposed to be doing things with
the Christian Union in some country hall.
But I've skipped their earnest Bible studies
and the same old frustrated prayers,

I find a stall selling incense, Indian
scarves, and statues of all the gods
you could ever wish to know.
Ganesh and Kali, a laughing Buddha, a votive

of Mary, Jesus and Joseph, a hand of Fatima,
blue charms against the evil eye,
the Eye of Horus carved into a two-pence coin,
a crystal that can help with water divination,

a pack of Tarot cards. My mother is close by
telling me not to listen to the Devil. *He likes
to present the alternatives with a silver tongue.*
But this Olympus on a trestle table does not

seem much fun. I look at all these fetishes
with a growing sense of vertigo,
while everything that was certain shifts on its axis.
The fog gets heavier, a shroud, or a dense mystery.

And as I turn the shadow of a tree,
faint around the edges, its map of branches,
flowing, the possibilities of my life unfolding,
against the pale expedience of the November sky.

Lot's Wife

So we left it, burning, and escaped – only just –
as the timbers fell behind us across the threshold.
Now that the End Times that you predicted are here
it looks like something from TV: Armageddon, Apocalypse,
full of explosions and grotesque decapitations.
I could feel the heat against my back
all the way up the mountain, a long climb and
difficult in the dark with the children clinging
to my ankles, the dead weight of all of my possessions.

I looked back because I wanted to be amazed
at how my old life could be turned to ruin,
to catch my breath, take a sip of water, but he had already run
on ahead. I was slow with all that I was carrying.
Perhaps I was surprised, too, by the size of the disaster.
A whole city burning, turning the sky into a late Monet,
the blind man's lurid colours, beautiful in the way that
transformations have of provoking wonder.
At first I thought it was the tears that I could taste,
or sweat, but then my legs began to go.

So here I am, traveller, watch and learn,
disaster stalks the unwary at every turn,
the trick is to keep moving while you can.

Glossary

Anws Blewog	Hairy anus
Chware	Playing
Cnawd	Flesh
Cer i grafu	Go and scratch
Ebol	Donkey
Ei phen	Your head
Fach	Little
Fy Ngheffyl ddu	My black horse
Gorsaf	Station
Gyrru	Driving/Speeding
Iechyd Da	Good health
Llaeth	Milk
Mwnci	Monkey
Marchogaeth	To ride – a horse, bicycle
Pregethwr	Preacher
Y Ddraig Coch	The Red Dragon
Un, dau, tri	One, two, three

Acknowledgements

'National Eisteddfod, Carmarthen, 1975' was first published in *New Welsh Reader*.

The epigraph for this book is taken from the poem 'To Church' by R.S. Thomas (first published in *Poetry* British Number edited by Charles Tomlinson, Volume 100 Number 2, Poetry Foundation, 1962).

This book has taken a while to compose and settle into the shape of this collection and there are many people who have helped it along the way. I'd like to thank especially Katy Evans-Bush and Susie Wildsmith for their editorial support. And along the way Gillian Clarke, Fran Lock, Emma Hargrave and my inestimable, Golnoosh Nour have all given me their support and love, this is for you, too.

So many of the poems are exploded memories:
An interview with Julia Bell

Julia Bell is a writer and academic. She is the author of novels, the bestselling *Creative Writing Coursebook* and the book-length essay *Radical Attention*. Her essays and short stories have been published nationally and internationally including in the *TLS*, the *White Review* and the *Paris Review* and broadcast on the BBC. Her poetry has been longlisted for the National Poetry Competition and the Bridport Prize. She is a Reader in Creative Writing at Birkbeck, University of London.

Late in the 1960s, before Bell was born, her father and mother visited Aberaeron, a small fishing town on the west coast of Wales. Here, her father heard a voice – which he knew to be God – directing him to minister to the Welsh. Six months after she was born in the early 1970s, they moved to Aberaeron where he took up his first curateship. Over the next eighteen years they would move to various parishes within a forty mile radius: first to Llangeler a predominantly Welsh-speaking parish in the Teifi valley, then back to Aberaeron where Bell's father became vicar, and then to a larger and more Evangelical church in Aberystwyth.

This unique memoir in verse offers a series of snapshots about religion and sexuality. In verse because it's how Bell remembers: snapshots in words strung along a line, which somehow constitute a life. Snapshots of another time from now, but from a time which tells us about how Bell got here. Not the whole story, but her story. Of an English family on a mission from God, of signs and wonders in the Welsh countryside, of difference, and of faith and its loss.

'Moving, tender writing with a haunting evocation of place and time.'
– Hannah Lowe

'These full-throated poems bring to resonant life the story of a daughter whose father's calling "sits on all our shoulders like a fog". Bewildered by severities at odds with her body, she wonders at Jonah breathing inside a whale while on land "I do not know which way is up … The surface is so far down." Yet the desires of the queer self unfolding in thrilling detail here refuse to be extinguished – the phrasing in *Hymnal* glistens with the rich clarity of stained glass.'
– John McCullough

What inspired you to write *Hymnal*?
I started writing *Hymnal* about ten years ago at Ty Newydd on a writing course with Gillian Clarke and Carol Ann Duffy. Gillian Clarke actually came to Aberaeron school when I was a teenager and did a writing class with us. It was in that class that I knew I wanted to be a writer and writing poetry was always part of what I did privately as I grew up and developed my career. So after focusing on fiction it was good to return to Wales and to write poetry again and perhaps inevitably the book started to take shape in those workshops in Llanystumdwy. Going back to the past seemed like a good place to begin with my poetic voice.

Tell us a little about the themes.
It's a memoir in verse so many of the poems are exploded memories – small snapshots in time, which is how I think my memory works. I arranged it in as linear order as I could. A publisher once suggested I write a version of it in narrative prose but I think this version is more true to my experience of life. It was quite an intense childhood – living above the shop as it were – always concerned with the big existential questions about life and death which I realised as I grew older wasn't the experience of other families. Add sexuality to that mix and I think I'm trying to explore and describe what it was like surrounded by the Bible and Hymns and the poetry of the Welsh language whilst also realising that I was gay. I'm trying to think through these things in the collection – religion and sexuality and the reality of queer desire in the 1980s in an age of Clause 28 etc.

What inspires you to write?
Everything – I mean, isn't everything poetry? But, to be more serious, I am inspired to write poetry in a different way than prose. I'm writing more non-fiction now which is inspired by wanting to describe and explain things to myself. With poetry I'm trying to unpack an image or an idea – or sometimes even a

phrase. At the moment I'm working on a new sequence of pieces about objects from the natural world that I collected as a child. Also, reading great work by other writers is always inspiring.

Who are some writers you admire?
In poetry I really love the work of Philip Larkin for its straightforwardness. But I also love R.S. Thomas for all the gnarly wrestling with god. And Emily Dickinson and Elizabeth Bishop just because. In terms of contemporary poets I admire the work of Dorriane Laux, Denise Riley, and Sharon Olds very much. And Richard Scott, Ocean Vuong, and Joelle Taylor also seem to me to be at the vanguard of a new queer poetic which is beautiful and moving and inspiring to read.

What would be some advice you would give to your younger self?
Write more poetry!

What is your writing process?
I try to write every day but have had a bit of a hiatus last year because I moved house which was hugely disruptive to my routine. I'm getting back in the saddle now drafting some new pieces and a new essay, but last year was a bit of a writing write-off. Life gets in the way, it happens. I was also really burned out from teaching and running an MA in Creative Writing through the pandemic from my garden shed…

What books are currently on your bedside table?
I've just read Michael Bracewell's amazing new novel *Unfinished Business* – the density and intensity of his minimal prose style is really impressive. I had to keep stopping to re-read it. I'm currently re-reading through Denise Riley's new collection *Lurex* and enjoying very much Kevin Brazil's essays in *Whatever Happened to Queer Happiness? On* the to be read pile and coming next is Brigitte Reimann's *Siblings* – published by Penguin Classics in a new translation from the German and some of Margaret Atwood's poetry in *Dearly*.

I like to have a mix of things on the go at once, usually some poetry, prose and non-fiction.

Julia Bell, Spring 2023

PARTHIAN *Poetry*

How to Carry Fire
Christina Thatcher
ISBN 978-1-912681-48-8
£9 | Paperback

'A dazzling array of poems both remarkable in
their ingenuity, and raw, unforgettable honesty.'
– Helen Calcutt

Sliced Tongue and
Pearl Cufflinks
Kittie Belltree
ISBN 978-1-912681-14-3
£9 | Paperback

'By turns witty and sophisticated, her writing shivers
with a suggestion of unease that is compelling.'
– Samantha Wynne-Rhydderch

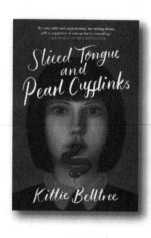

Hey Bert
Roberto Pastore
ISBN 978-1-912109-34-0
£9 | Paperback

'Bert's writing, quite simply, makes me happy.
Jealous but happy.'
– Crystal Jeans

PARTHIAN *Poetry*

The Language of Bees
Rae Howells
ISBN 978-1-913640-69-9
£9 | Paperback
'rich in love, for the world that we are inseparable from
and on the verge of destroying.'
– **Matthew Francis**

Small
Natalie Ann Holborow
ISBN 978-1-912681-76-1
£9.99 | Paperback

'Shoot for the moon? Holborow has landed, roamed its face,
dipped into the craters, and gathered an armful of stars
while up there.'
– *Wales Arts Review*

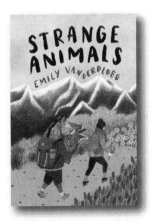

Strange Animals
Emily Vanderploeg
ISBN 978-1-913640-70-5
£9 | Paperback

'Emily Vanderploeg's clear-eyed lyric poetry explores the
questions of where we belong, who we have become, and who
or what undertakes that journey alongside us.'
– **Carolyn Smart**

PARTHIAN *Poetry*

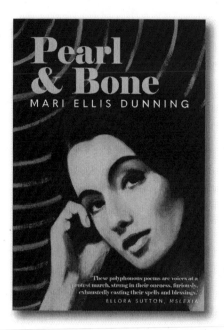

Pearl and Bone
Mari Ellis Dunning
ISBN 978-1-913640-72-9
£9 | Paperback

'These polyphonous poems are voices at a protest march, strong in their oneness, furiously, exhaustedly casting their spells and blessings.'
– Ellora Sutton, *Mslexia*

Beautiful, emotional and richly imagistic, Mari Ellis Dunning presents mothers in many forms: those experienced, chosen, unwitting, and presumed, asking us to consider the true nuances of motherhood – delicate as pearl, durable as bone.

Moon Jellyfish Can Barely Swim
Ness Owen
ISBN 978-1-913640-97-2
£10 | Paperback

'Form and feeling combine to create a collection which rewards the reader with a mesmerising portrait of a much-loved landscape brimming with startling imagery.'
– Samantha Wynne-Rhydderch

Moon jellyfish live a life adrift. Owen's second collection explores what it is to subsist with whatever the tides bring. Poems that journey from family to politics, womanhood and language.